LEVEL 2 ★★

Skunk Trunk

by Pearl Markovics

Consultant:
Beth Gambro
Reading Specialist
Yorkville, Illinois

Contents

BEARPORT
PUBLISHING

New York, New York

Skunk Trunk

Let's rhyme!

Here is some **junk**.

This is a big,
smelly **chunk**.

6

That **chunk** of **junk stunk.**

There goes a **skunk**!

First, it
hid under
a **bunk**.

Then, it ran up
a tree **trunk**.

The **skunk** also **stunk.**
It **stunk** worse than
the **junk**!

Key Words in the -unk Family

bunk

chunk

junk

skunk

stunk

trunk

Other **-unk** Words:
dunk, flunk, funk, sunk

Index

About the Author

Pearl Markovics enjoys having fun with words. She especially likes witty wordplay.

Teaching Tips

Before Reading

✔ Introduce rhyming words and the **–unk** word family to readers.

✔ Guide readers on a "picture walk" through the text by asking them to name the things shown.

✔ Discuss book structure by showing children where text will appear consistently on pages. Highlight the supportive pattern of the book.

During Reading

✔ Encourage readers to "read with your finger" and point to each word as it is read. Stop periodically to ask children to point to a specific word in the text.

✔ Reading strategies: When encountering unknown words, prompt readers with encouraging cues such as:

- **Does that word look like a word you already know?**
- **Does it rhyme with another word you have already read?**

After Reading

✔ Write the key words on index cards.

- **Have readers match them to pictures in the book.**

✔ Ask readers to identify their favorite page in the book. Have them read that page aloud.

✔ Choose an **–unk** word. Ask children to pick a word that rhymes with it.

✔ Ask children to create their own rhymes using **–unk** words. Encourage them to use the same pattern found in the book.

Credits: Cover, © Eric Isselee/Shutterstock and © Petoranong/Shutterstock; 2–3, © Wawritto/Shutterstock and © porjai kittawornrat/Shutterstock; 4–5, © porjai kittawornrat/Shutterstock and © givaga/Shutterstock; 6–7, © porjai kittawornrat/Shutterstock, © irin-k/Shutterstock, © Boonchuay1970/Shutterstock, © Lucia Fox/Shutterstock, and © Eric Isselee/Shutterstock; 8–9, © Eric Isselee/Shutterstock; 10–11, © Eric Isselee/Shutterstock and © Scott-lee/Shutterstock; 12–13, © Eric Isselee/Shutterstock, © xpixel/Shutterstock, and © LilKar/Shutterstock; 14–15, © Ultrashock/Shutterstock and © Johannes Kornelius/Shutterstock; 16T (L to R), © Scott-lee/Shutterstock, © porjai kittawornrat/Shutterstock, and © wawritto/Shutterstock; 16B (L to R), © Eric Isselee/Shutterstock, © Ultrashock/Shutterstock, and © xpixel/Shutterstock.

Publisher: Kenn Goin   **Senior Editor**: Joyce Tavolacci   **Creative Director**: Spencer Brinker

Library of Congress Cataloging-in-Publication Data: Names: Markovics, Pearl, author. | Gambro, Beth, consultant. Title: Skunk trunk / by Pearl Markovics; consultant: Beth Gambro, Reading Specialist, Yorkville, Illinois. Description: New York, New York: Bearport Publishing, [2020] | Series: Read and rhyme: Level 2 | Includes index. Identifiers: LCCN 2019007622 (print) | LCCN 2019012645 (ebook) | ISBN 9781642806045 (ebook) | ISBN 9781642805505 (library) | ISBN 9781642807165 (pbk.) Subjects: LCSH: Readers (Primary) Classification: LCC PE1119 (ebook) | LCC PE1119 .M28593 2020 (print) | DDC 428.6/2—dc23 LC record available at https://lccn.loc.gov/2019007622

10 9 8 7 6 5 4 3 2 1